GHOSTS OF THE White House

by Tammy Gagne

CAPSTONE PRESS
a capstone imprint

Bright Idea Books are published by Capstone Press
1710 Roe Crest Drive, North Mankato, Minnesota 56003
www.mycapstone.com

Library of Congress Cataloging-in-Publication Data
Names: Gagne, Tammy, author.
Title: Ghosts of the White House / by Tammy Gagne.
Description: North Mankato : Capstone Press, 2019. | Series: Ghosts and hauntings | Includes bibliographical references and index.
Identifiers: LCCN 2018018703 (print) | LCCN 2018020811 (ebook) | ISBN 9781543541908 (ebook) | ISBN 9781543541502 (hardcover : alk. paper)
Subjects: LCSH: White House (Washington, D.C.)--Miscellanea--Juvenile literature. | Ghosts--Washington (D.C.)--Juvenile literature. | Haunted houses--Washington (D.C.)--Juvenile literature.
Classification: LCC BF1472.U6 (ebook) | LCC BF1472.U6 G34 2019 (print) | DDC 133.109753--dc23
LC record available at https://lccn.loc.gov/2018018703

Editorial Credits
Editor: Maddie Spalding
Designer: Becky Daum
Production Specialist: Melissa Martin

Photo Credits
AP Images: Gerald Herbert, 18–19; iStockphoto: JTSorrell, 30–31; Library of Congress: Detroit Photographic Company/Library of Congress, 10–11, Jack E. Boucher/Library of Congress, 24–25; Shutterstock Images: Andrea Izzotti, 5, AR Pictures, cover (background), Everett Art, 6–7, 8, Everett Historical, cover (foreground), 13, 14–15, 17, 21, 28, flysnowfly, 26–27, Olga Popova, 22–23

Design Elements: iStockphoto, Red Line Editorial, and Shutterstock Images

TABLE OF CONTENTS

CHAPTER 1

ABIGAIL Adams

Many people think the White House is **haunted**. Some say they have seen the ghosts of presidents. Others say they have seen the ghosts of **first ladies**.

Some people have reported seeing the ghost of Abigail Adams. Abigail was married to John Adams. He was the second U.S. president.

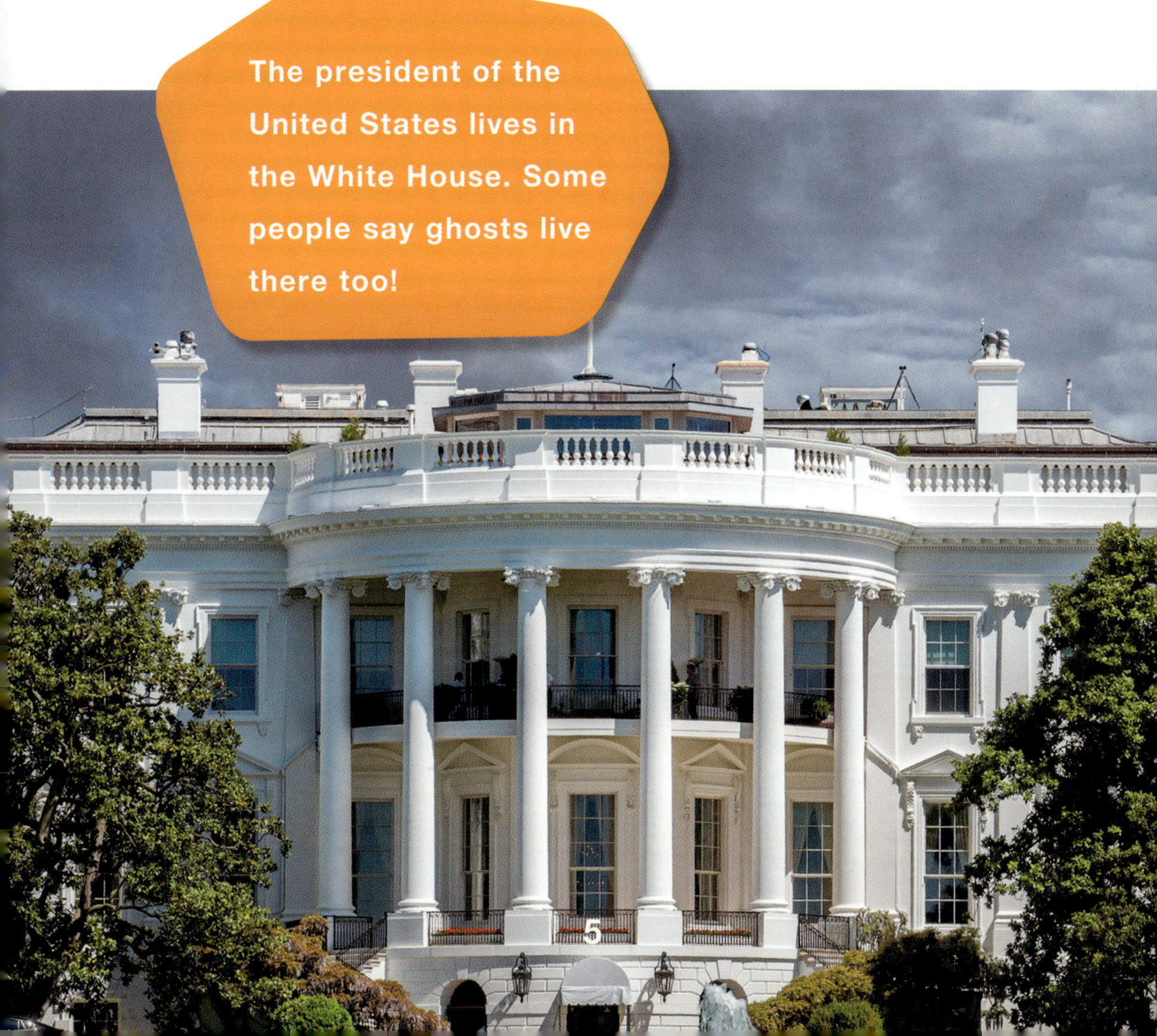

The president of the United States lives in the White House. Some people say ghosts live there too!

The White House was mostly completed in 1800. Then Abigail and John moved in. They were the first president and first lady to live there.

Some people think they've seen the ghost of Abigail Adams in the White House.

John Adams was president from 1797 to 1801.

Abigail and John moved to Massachusetts in 1801. Abigail fell ill with fever in 1818. She died in her home. But her ghost seems to haunt the White House.

ABIGAIL'S GHOST

Abigail's ghost was first seen in the early 1900s. People say she wears a lace hat and a shawl.

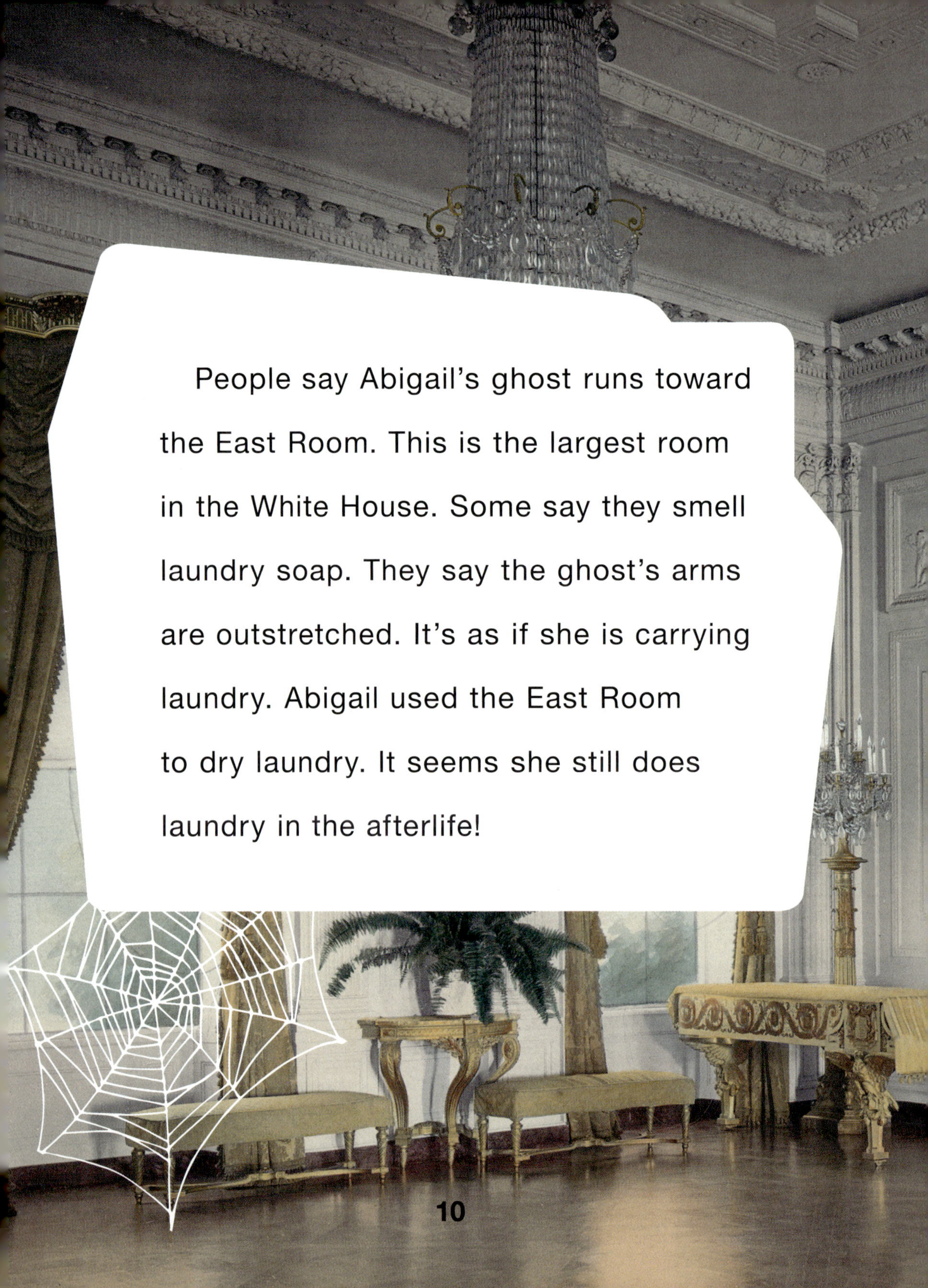

People say Abigail's ghost runs toward the East Room. This is the largest room in the White House. Some say they smell laundry soap. They say the ghost's arms are outstretched. It's as if she is carrying laundry. Abigail used the East Room to dry laundry. It seems she still does laundry in the afterlife!

The East Room has been redecorated many times since John and Abigail Adams lived in the White House.

CHAPTER 2

ANDREW Jackson

Have you ever heard a ghost laughing? Some White House guests say they have. They spent the night in the Rose Room. An old bed is kept there. It belonged to President Andrew Jackson. Jackson died in 1845. Visitors have since been awakened by someone laughing.

Some people have heard stomping. Others have heard an angry voice. They think this is Jackson's ghost.

Andrew Jackson was president from 1829 to 1837.

Jackson ran for president in 1824. His **rival** was John Quincy Adams. John Quincy was the son of John and Abigail Adams. The race was close. But John Quincy won. Jackson became president four years later. But he remained upset by the loss. Some people say his ghost is still mad about this.

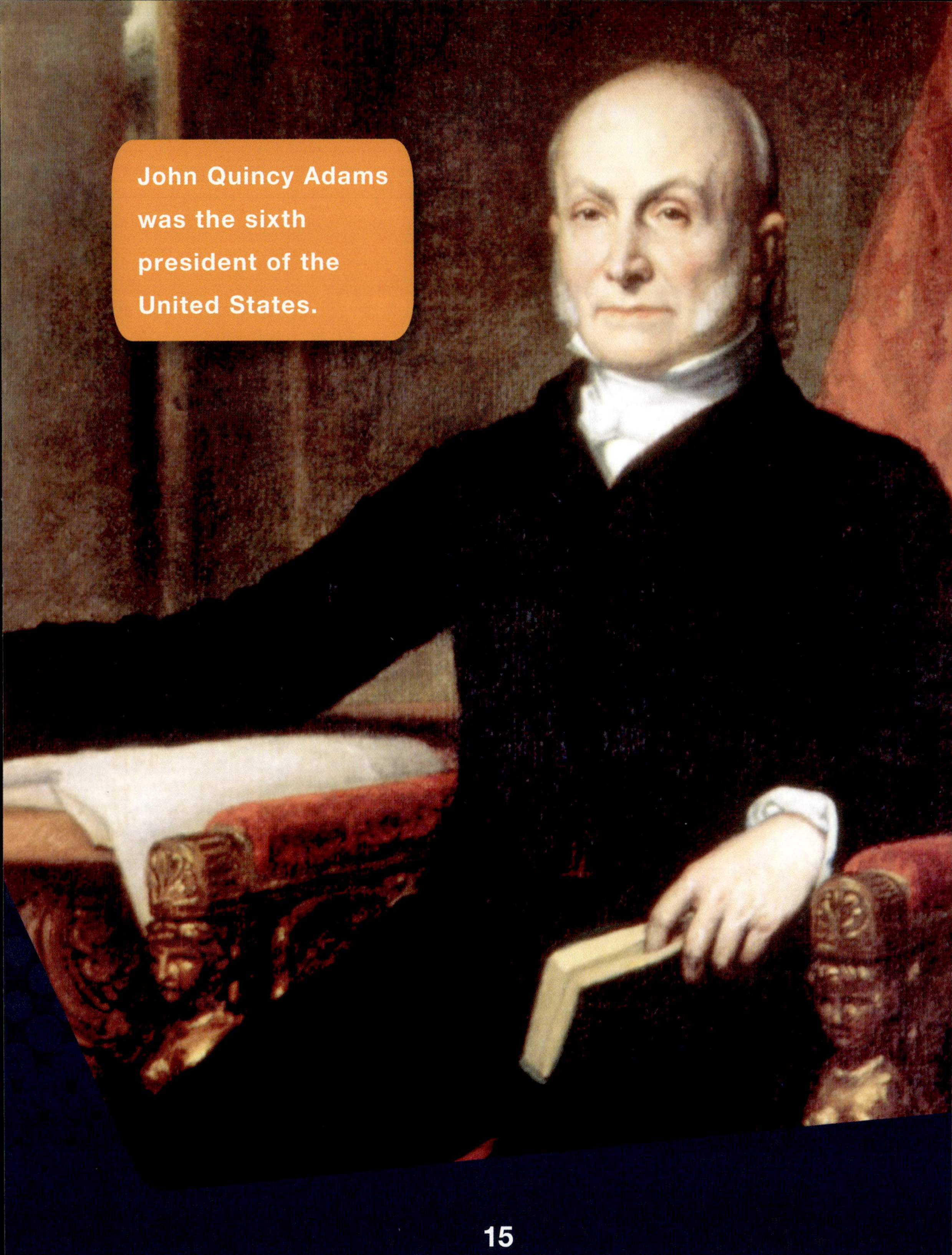

John Quincy Adams was the sixth president of the United States.

CHAPTER 3

DOLLEY Madison

First lady Edith Wilson had a project planned. It was the early 1900s. Edith was married to President Woodrow Wilson. Edith wanted to change the White House's Rose Garden. But her gardeners quit. They said a ghost scared them.

They believed the ghost was Dolley Madison. Dolley was a former first lady. She had planted the garden 100 years earlier.

Dolley Madison hosted many parties during her time as first lady.

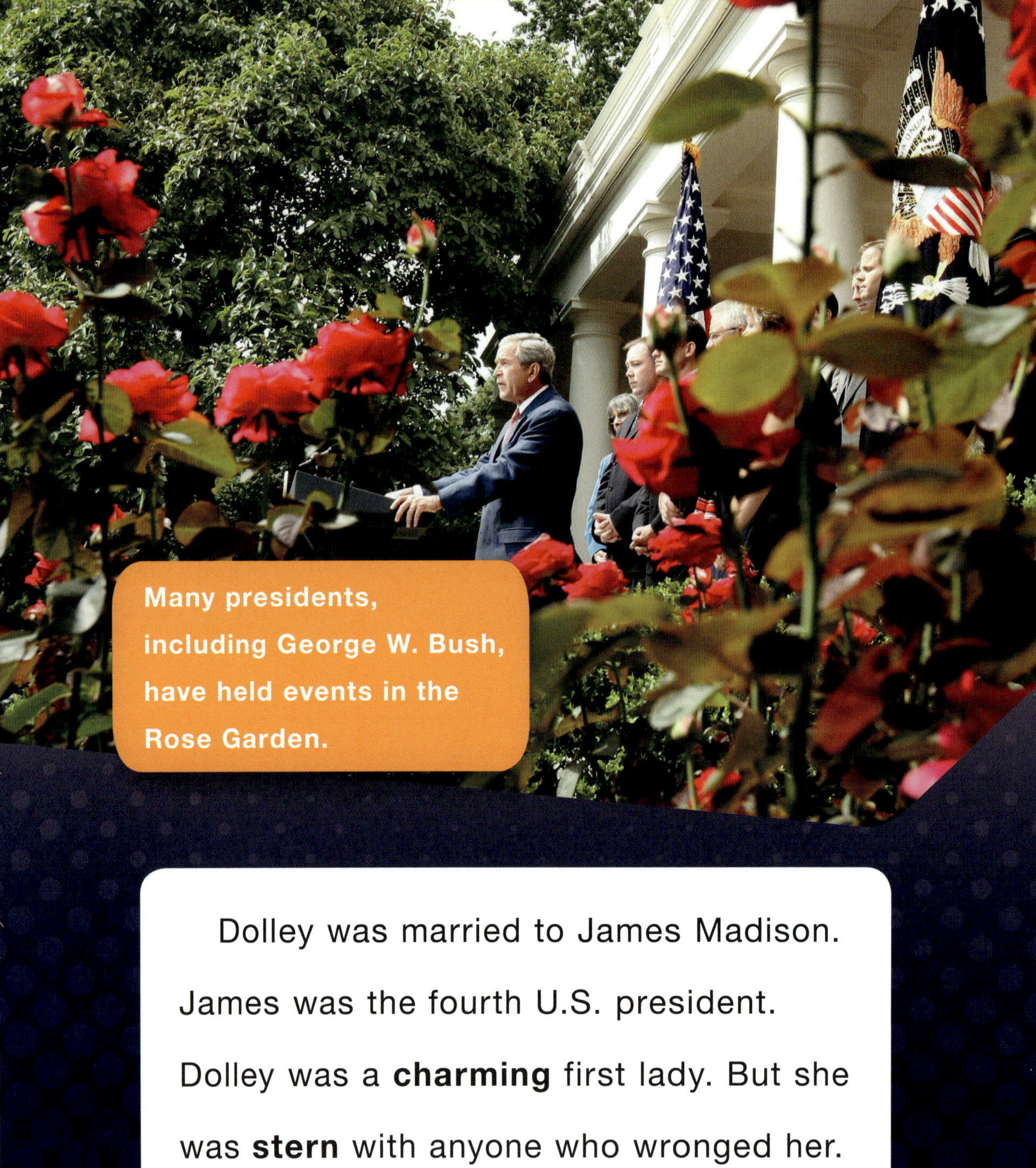

Many presidents, including George W. Bush, have held events in the Rose Garden.

Dolley was married to James Madison. James was the fourth U.S. president. Dolley was a **charming** first lady. But she was **stern** with anyone who wronged her. It seems her ghost is no different.

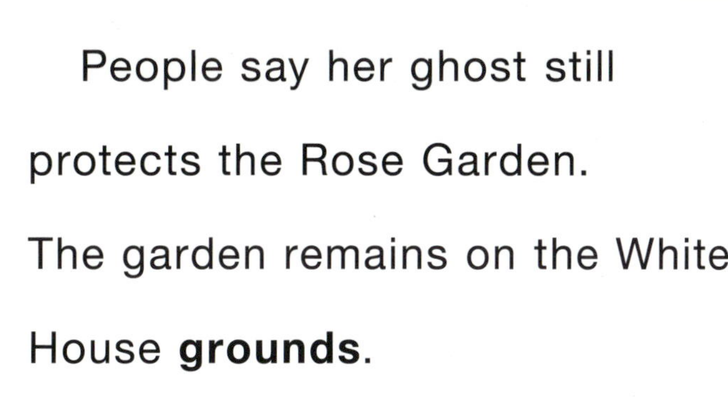

People say her ghost still protects the Rose Garden. The garden remains on the White House **grounds**.

SAVING ARTWORK

British soldiers burned down the White House in 1814. Dolley saved a painting of President George Washington. The White House was later rebuilt.

CHAPTER 4

THE LINCOLN Ghosts

President Abraham Lincoln died in 1865. He was killed at Ford's Theatre in Washington, D.C. But some people say his ghost haunts the White House.

The White House has 16 guest rooms. Guests stay in these rooms. One room is the Lincoln Bedroom. Lincoln used this room as an office. Some people have reported seeing his ghost in this room.

Abraham Lincoln was the 16th president of the United States.

Former British prime minister Winston Churchill said he talked to Lincoln's ghost.

Winston Churchill visited the White House in the 1940s. Churchill was the British **prime minister**. He was taking a bath. He walked into the Lincoln Bedroom after his bath. He saw a figure by the fireplace. The figure looked like Lincoln.

REAGAN'S DOG

President Ronald Reagan's dog wouldn't go into the Lincoln Bedroom. Some people think the dog saw Lincoln's ghost!

Churchill was not the only person to see Lincoln's ghost. Others have reported sightings in the Lincoln Bedroom. They say they saw Lincoln's ghost putting on boots.

The furniture in the Lincoln Bedroom was purchased by Abraham Lincoln's wife, Mary.

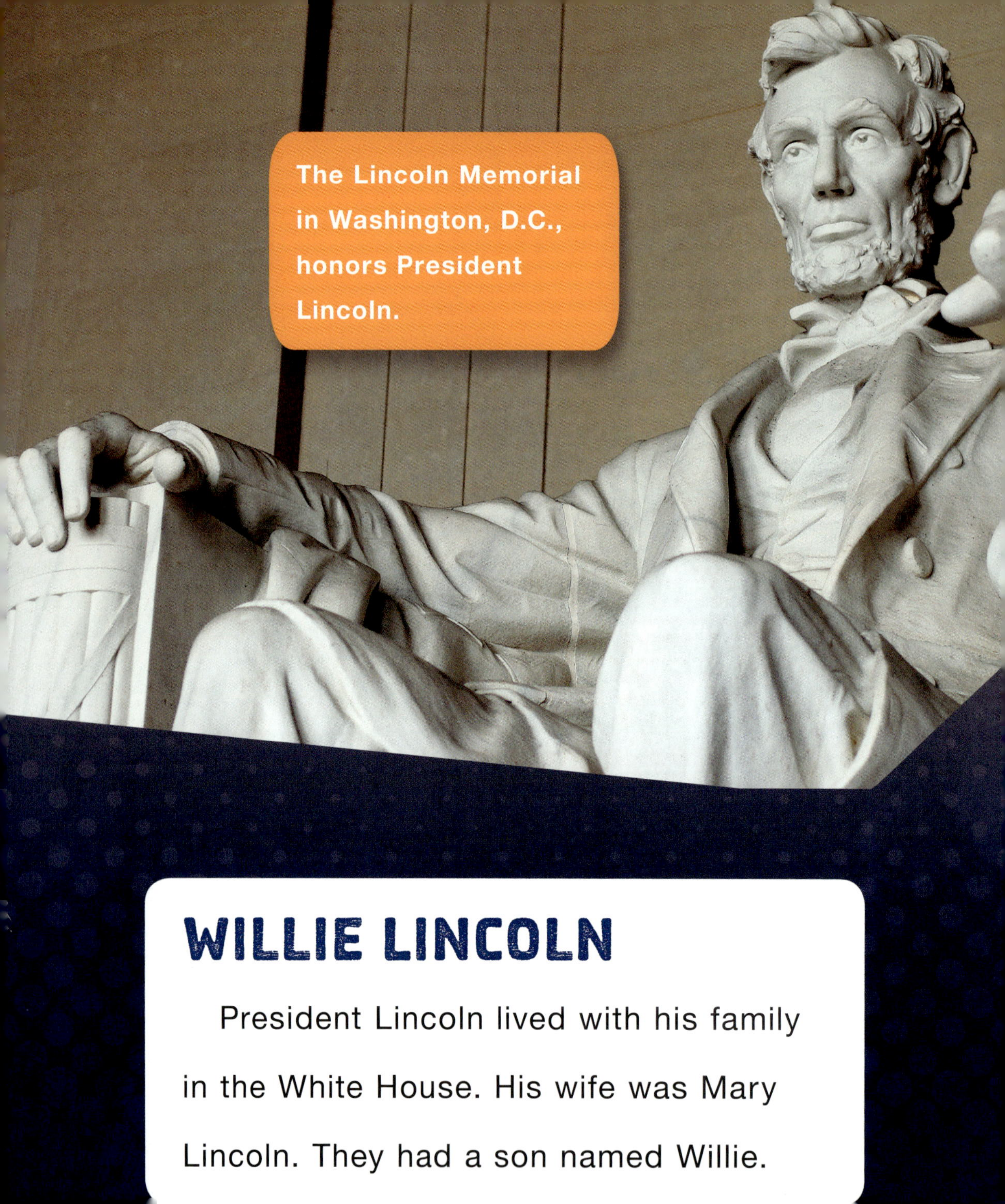

The Lincoln Memorial in Washington, D.C., honors President Lincoln.

WILLIE LINCOLN

President Lincoln lived with his family in the White House. His wife was Mary Lincoln. They had a son named Willie.

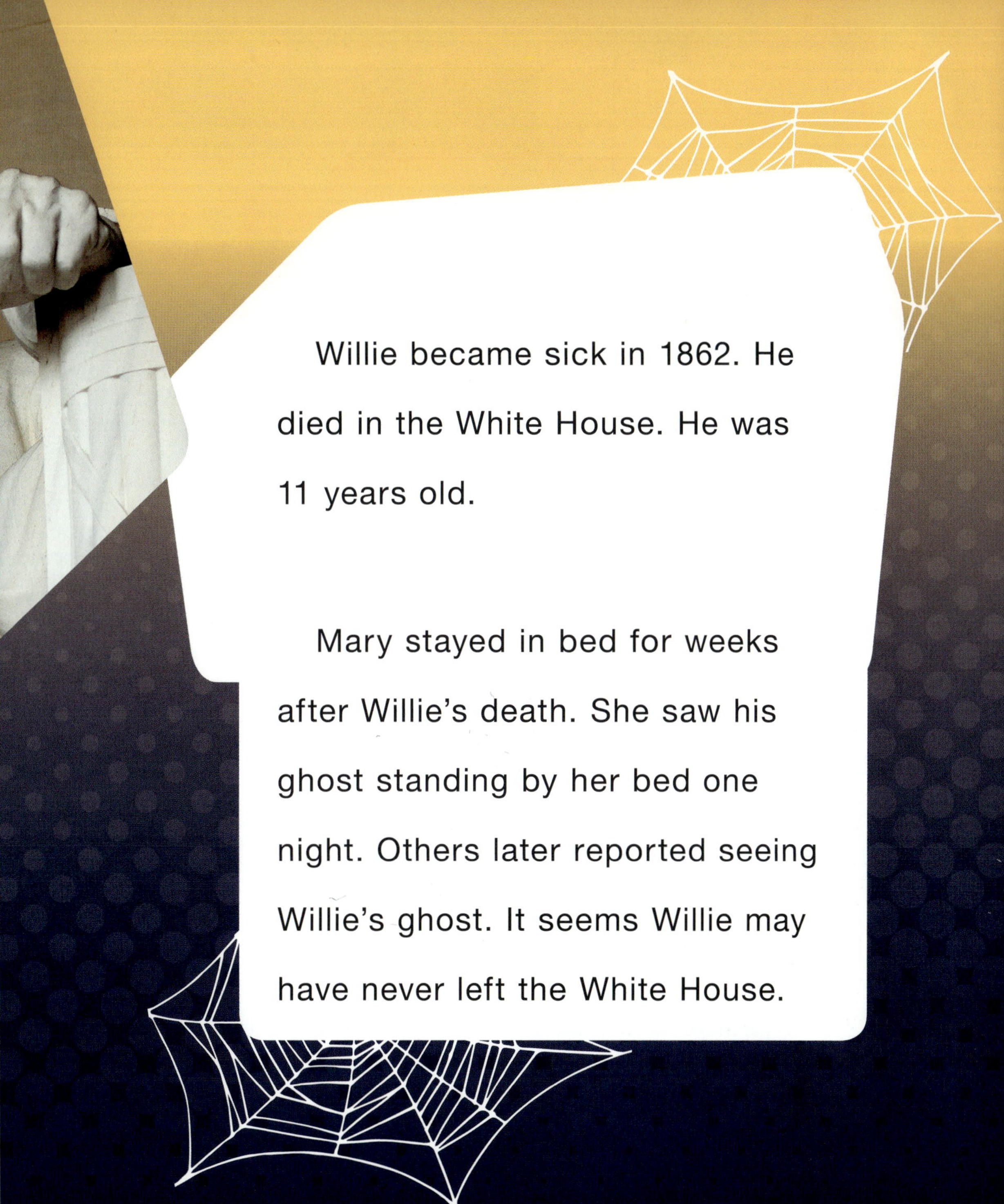

Willie became sick in 1862. He died in the White House. He was 11 years old.

Mary stayed in bed for weeks after Willie's death. She saw his ghost standing by her bed one night. Others later reported seeing Willie's ghost. It seems Willie may have never left the White House.

GLOSSARY

charming
pleasing or delightful

first lady
the wife of a U.S. president

grounds
the property surrounding a house

haunted
having mysterious events happen often, possibly due to visits from ghosts

prime minister
the ruler of the government in some countries

rival
a person that someone competes against

shawl
clothing that covers a person's head or shoulders

stern
serious and unfriendly

1. Grace Coolidge was the first person to see Abraham Lincoln's ghost. Grace was first lady in the 1920s. She was married to President Calvin Coolidge. She reported seeing Lincoln's ghost in the Oval Office. The Oval Office is the president's office. Grace said she saw the ghost looking out a window.

2. William Henry Harrison was the first president to die in the White House. He died in 1841. People have heard noises in the White House's attic. They say this is Harrison's ghost.

3. President Thomas Jefferson enjoyed playing the violin. He played in the White House's Yellow Oval Room. Jefferson died in 1826. Some people have since heard violin music coming from this room. They claim Jefferson's ghost is playing the music.

ACTIVITY

Research one of the ghosts in this book. Create a movie based on the life of the person you researched. You may use a video camera or a smartphone to film your movie.

You can use friends or family as characters in your movie. Act out an important event in the person's life. What new information did you learn?

FURTHER RESOURCES

To discover more White House haunting stories, explore these resources:

The History Channel: Ghosts in the White House
http://www.history.com/topics/halloween/ghosts-in-the-white-house

Owings, Lisa. *Ghosts in the White House.* Minneapolis, Minn.: Bellwether Media, 2017.

The White House Historical Association: White House Ghost Stories
https://www.whitehousehistory.org/press-room/press-fact-sheets/white-house-ghost-stories

Would you like to learn more about the history of the White House? Check out these books:

Clay, Kathryn. *The White House: Introducing Primary Sources.* North Mankato, Minn.: Capstone Press, 2018.

Flynn, Sarah Wassner. *1,000 Facts About the White House.* Washington, D.C.: National Geographic, 2017.

INDEX